WHAT OTHERS ARE SAYING

Tricia offers powerful words of encouragement and *hope* for all who experience depression and anxiety on this life journey. She provides a candid look into her journal and reflections on what helped her find her way out of her mental crisis. Crediting God's blessings of scripture, medicine, and faith, she is living proof of HOPE for healing amid the mental health crisis many face today.
—Amy Patterson, MSW

Tricia Opitz candidly shares her struggles with anxiety and depression, a rapidly growing societal issue affecting all ages. She offers devotions, suggested activities, and journaling pages to support and guide those who battle these mental health issues. While there are no quick fixes, Tricia's insights provide a valuable tool to help others cope with these challenges.
—Mary Strong, Retired School Administrator

Tricia's journey through the valley of mental illness shines a light into the darkness of troubled minds. Her message touched my heart, as it will so many amid the chaos and distress of our current world. I don't know anyone who isn't suffering from overwhelm and often defeat. Tricia breathes hope into our weary souls. I highly recommend her book to every peace-seeking individual. You will be mightily encouraged!
—Andrea Lende, Best-Selling Author, Speaker, Writing Coach

PANIC
to
PEACE

30 Days of Hope

Tricia Opitz

BEATITUDES LLC

© 2023 Panic to Peace by Tricia Opitz

All rights reserved.

No portion of this book may be reproduced in any form without written permission from the publisher or author, except as permitted by U.S. copyright law.

Contact Tricia Opitz with requests for permission to quote from this book at P.O. Box 542, Pryor, OK 74362, or via e-mail at triciajots4Jesus@triciajots4Jesus.com.

All Scripture quotations, unless otherwise indicated, are taken from the Holy Bible, New International Version®, NIV®. Copyright ©1973, 1978, 1984, 2011 by Biblica, Inc.® Used by permission of Zondervan. All rights reserved worldwide. www.zondervan.com The "NIV" and "New International Version" are trademarks registered in the United States Patent and Trademark Office by Biblica, Inc.®

Scripture quotations marked AMPC are taken from the Amplified® Bible, Copyright © 1954, 1958, 1962, 1964, 1965, 1987 by The Lockman Foundation. Used by permission. lockman.org

Scripture quotations marked NKJV are taken from the New King James Version®. Copyright © 1982 by Thomas Nelson. Used by permission. All rights reserved.

Scripture quotations marked NLT are taken from the *Holy Bible*, New Living Translation, copyright ©1996, 2004, 2015 by Tyndale House Foundation. Used by permission of Tyndale House Publishers, Carol Stream, Illinois 60188. All rights reserved.

Scripture quotations marked BSB are taken from The Holy Bible, Berean Study Bible. Copyright ©2016, 2020 by Bible Hub. Used by Permission. All Rights Reserved Worldwide. bereanbible.com

ISBN: 978-1-962581-10-3
ISBN: 978-1-962581-11-0

Cover & Interior Design by Ruth Hovsepian
Illustrations by VictoriyaD and AlteaDesign at Canva.com

To God Almighty,
Maker of heaven and earth,
from whom all healing comes.

And to my husband, Michael Opitz,
who has faithfully loved me
through all my ups and downs.

ACKNOWLEDGEMENTS

I'm grateful to you, **Mike Opitz**, my husband, for your support throughout this project.

My deepest gratitude to the many who prayed for me, especially my telephone prayer partner, **Rebecca Bogers**, my ladies' group prayer partner, **Wilma Vaughan** and all those who lifted hearts to heaven on my behalf as I worked on this book.

Many thanks to **Andrea Lende**, who encouraged me repeatedly and helped me publish this book.

I'm grateful to **Jennie Burgardt**, who took the photo of me for this book.

Thank you, **Lyneta Smith**, for your excellent editing work, clear explanations, and encouragement.

Thank you, **Ruth Hovsepian**, for your formatting and book design and for sharing your technical expertise in the Beatitudes Self-Publishing group.

FOREWORD

Hope is to our spirits what oxygen is to our lungs. Lose hope, and you die. They may not bury you for a while, but without hope, you are dead inside. The only way to face the future is to fly straight into it on the wings of hope... Hope is the energy of the soul. Hope is the power of tomorrow. -Lewis B. Smedes

Tricia has found her way through the darkness of hopelessness, seeing the light at the end of the tunnel and then finding wings to lift her higher as she found strength, guidance, and comfort in the Lord. Her journey is reflected in these devotions and can guide others along the path of hope.

As Tricia's pastor over the years, I know she has struggled, and depression is real. Her longing is to be free of the torment that comes with the dark cloud and enjoy the sunlit meadows of God's grace. She has overcome so much and continues to experience more of the joys of the Lord. What she shares has been forged on the anvil of experience and enlightened by the light of the Lord.

Randy Huddleston
Pastor, Grace Bible Church
P.O. Box 332, Pryor, OK 74362
pastor@gracebiblepryor.org

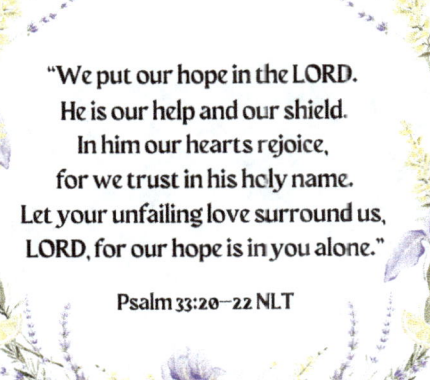

"We put our hope in the LORD.
He is our help and our shield.
In him our hearts rejoice,
for we trust in his holy name.
Let your unfailing love surround us,
LORD, for our hope is in you alone."

Psalm 33:20–22 NLT

Contents

BEFORE YOU BEGIN

I HAD DRIVEN ABOUT a half mile home from my in-laws' house. Suddenly, I felt panicked—weak, trembling, sweaty palms, dry mouth, unable to keep driving. What was I afraid of? Maybe I feared that I couldn't keep the car on the road or would faint and have a wreck. But the fear disabled me, and I called my husband for help.

Does panic ever paralyze you? My prayer is that you will find hope and healing within these pages.

Symptoms of depression and anxiety vary. Yours may differ from mine. One time, I felt weepy with almost constant panic and chest pains. In my first experience with panic attacks (also called anxiety attacks), the doctor put me in the hospital with a diagnosis of depression. At other times, weakness and fear dominated my experience.

You may know that anxiety and depression can come together or separately, debilitating a person. Either way, we suffer miserably during them.

I've found no easy answers, but that doesn't mean we should give up. There is help and hope whenever we proceed on a journey toward wholeness and whatever our location along the path. I wrote the devotions in this book during times of panic and depression. In them, I offer you the comfort with which God comforted me.

The devotion for each day includes a "next step" to help you along your journey toward peace. I've included a journal page with each one because journaling helps us get our swirling thoughts out of our heads and onto paper where we can see them. I encourage you to use that page to respond to the "Next Step" suggestion and to write down your thoughts, feelings, and prayers.

I suggest you progress through the book at a leisurely pace, not more than one devotion per day, because in depression we often struggle just to get out of bed. Give God time to speak to your heart and comfort your soul.

I've written about the hope and healing I found in the following pages. God will help you find encouragement as you read on.

1

HOPE AMID ANXIETY

DEPRESSION HAS HOUNDED ME for most of my life, with a breakdown in 1988 being the first time doctors diagnosed it.

Then, a few years ago, medication problems threw me into another bout with anxiety and depression (which often go together). Since I love God and have been a Christ follower for many years, I thought I would be exempt from such difficulties. Sometimes, people in the church believe those suffering from mental or emotional problems need more faith. However, depression and anxiety can attack anyone, Christian or not, faith-filled or not.

For me, medicine, counseling, and other therapies have helped.

Sometimes, I tried to function without the medicine, hoping that extra Bible reading or prayer would solve my problems. But I couldn't do it. It is beautiful to draw near God, but taking advantage of appropriate medication or other therapies can make a big difference. I praise God for all the help I receive because He is the source of every good thing.

If God chose to, He could heal me, and I wouldn't need medicine. But maybe that's not God's priority work in my life currently. He is sovereign and trustworthy. So, I thank God for enabling people to develop medicines to help with these problems. I'm also very thankful for the many people who prayed for me and loved me through that struggle and for the Scriptures that encouraged me and gave me hope.

For example, I love Psalm 62:5 in the Amplified Bible, Classic Edition (AMPC), which says, "My soul, wait only upon God and silently submit to Him; for my hope and expectation are from Him."

Next Step: Write down anything that has helped you so far through your anxiety or depression. Thank God for this help He has given you.

Prayer: *Gracious Father, sometimes I forget to submit to You humbly and gratefully. Let Your Holy Spirit remind me. Amen.*

2

A RAY OF HOPE

A JOURNAL ENTRY IN the valley:

"I have a doctor's appointment at 9:00, and I'm supposed to drive to my husband's workplace to pick him up so he can go with me. Unreasonable fear has tormented me day and night for some time now. My thoughts tumble in a hamster wheel of wondering what is wrong with me, fearing that I might faint and no one could help me. Chest pains started early last week. My body feels so weak! I can't make my feet step out the door. I'll have to call my husband and tell him I can't drive this morning, and he will need to come get me."

That happened on a Monday morning about thirty-five years ago. I still remember the panic, uncontrollable crying, body weakness, sweaty palms, and trembling during the months leading up to that day. When the panic attacks (as I later learned they were called) first started, they came only occasionally. Then, they started happening more and more frequently. Finally, they had become constant when the chest pains began.

At the appointment that morning, the doctor recommended a hospital stay and referred me to a psychiatrist who prescribed an antidepressant and an "as-needed" sedative. The antidepressant helped, and I didn't need the sedative often. After a few days, a Christian couple I knew visited me in the hospital and prayed for me.

The following day, I felt like God slipped a ray of hope into my heart where I had felt hopeless and helpless. Maybe I could get well after all.

And I did get well. It took some time, and I still need an antidepressant, but I am free of panic attacks and depression.

"Why, my soul, are you downcast? Why so disturbed within me? Put your hope in God, for I will yet praise him, my Savior and my God." (Psalm 42:11)

Next Step: Write down an area where you need a ray of hope today. You can call on our compassionate God. He listens and understands your pain.

Prayer: Compassionate Father, please shine Your love into the parts of my heart that feel hopeless and helpless today. Thank You for Your love and mercy. Amen.

3

GOD WILL LIFT YOU UP

"THIS MEDICINE DOESN'T HELP me, and besides, it makes my mouth so dry that no matter how much water I drink, it's not enough. I've taken it for a few weeks, and it hasn't made any difference."

That's what I thought about the medicine that the doctor at the mental health clinic prescribed. I continued going to the clinic for counseling but didn't mention that I quit taking the meds. The counseling alone wasn't enough to handle my problems, and I stopped going. My husband thought a daily walk outside was what I needed. We walked together once a day—I was afraid to walk alone.

That was before I landed in the hospital with depression. Counseling, exercise, and medicine are helpful but not enough individually. In the hospital, I had no choice but to take the medicine. Although we didn't go outside, we received group and individual counseling and walked daily in an exercise room.

I wonder if I would have gotten well without the hospital stay if I had seen and heeded 1 Peter 5:6, which says, "Humble yourselves, therefore, under God's mighty hand, that he may lift you up in due time." Had I remembered that verse, would I have recognized the medicine as God's hand?

Maybe so, but the reality is that I was hospitalized, and God used that for His purposes.

Next Step: Write a prayer asking God to reveal what He wants you to submit to Him.

Prayer: All-wise, Father, please help me recognize when You are calling me to humble myself under Your mighty hand. Amen.

4

A Journey Begins

"Your sodium level is low, and the antidepressant medicine you're taking is known for causing low sodium," the doctor said. "I suggest you get off this medicine and try a different one if you still need an antidepressant."

So, I stepped down on the dosage until I was off that medication. I prayed, read my Bible, read devotionals, continued daily exercise, spent quiet time with the Lord, and asked others to pray for me (which they did).

Nevertheless, sleeping problems started in the first week without the medicine. I woke up frequently in the night with sweaty palms and panic. During the day, my insides felt like jelly, and my hands trembled constantly. Soon, fear and self-doubt took over my mind. My thoughts flew into a whirlwind, thinking of failures, not good enough, should have, ought to, God expects better, others are better, and on and on.

I returned to my doctor, who prescribed different medicines, which didn't help. I finally checked into a local hospital. The doctor put me back on the antidepressant that had previously worked. I spent Christmas in the hospital that year. After a couple of weeks, I felt ready to go home.

But at home, I felt overwhelmed by the simplest tasks. I slept only two hours at a time during the night, waking up in panic between "naps." At first, I struggled to get up in the mornings. I felt devastated by anxiety and thought I couldn't face the day. But I did get up each morning and spent time with Jesus. I attended church weekly.

I thought I should feel better right away. Instead, symptoms dragged on for months.

Psalm 33:20–22 reminds us to put our hope in God alone and that He is our help and shield. Jeremiah 17:7 points out that people who trust and hope in God are blessed.

Sometimes, the encouraging Bible verses I read and put in my journal didn't seem helpful or encouraging. I didn't feel less anxious. But as I kept writing verses, God placed little grains of peace into my soul.

Next Step: Write down the anxiety or depression symptoms that bother you most. Ask God to help you, and then look through the Bible verses listed in Appendix 1 in the back of this book to find Scriptures that will comfort you. Write down a few of these also.

Prayer: God, our hope and help and shield, please sustain me with Your unfailing love when nothing seems to help.

5

GOD SENDS COMFORT

FROM THE BEGINNING OF this struggle with anxiety, God sent me comfort in Scripture verses.

"The Lord is good, a refuge in times of trouble. He cares for those who trust in Him" (Nahum 1:7).

"The Lord is gracious and righteous; our God is full of compassion. ... Return to your rest, my soul, for the Lord has been good to you" (Psalm 116:5, 7).

I wrote these and many others in my journal, but I also wrote:

"The feelings of anxiety are so strong that my mind can't seem to grasp this comfort. In anxiety mode, I feel unable to believe or trust. I feel like I can't hold onto the truth."

Maybe I couldn't hold onto the truth, but God held onto me. When I believed in Jesus Christ as God's Son and committed my life to Him, God made me His child (John 1:12–13). At that time, God took me into His hands and never let me go. He promises that He never will (John 10:28-29), and He keeps all His promises.

My feelings can't change the truth of God's Word. Neither can my self-doubts, sweaty palms, trembling body, or overwhelming panic change the reality of God's secure hold on me. Because I had trouble believing that in my journey through Anxiety Valley, I'm thankful for our pastor, who reminded me of this truth when I needed to hear it. And since I'm feeling better now, I offer it as hope to those who are feeling the way I did.

Is your heart having trouble believing what your mind knows is true? Take courage. Even when we can't hold onto the truth, Jesus, who is the Truth, holds onto us.

Next Step: Find one of God's promises that gives you hope today. Write it down and meditate on it. Feel free to use one of those referenced above, which helped me.

Prayer: *Thank You for Your promise not to forsake me, no matter what, faithful Father. (Hebrews 13:5.)*

6

GUILTY OR NOT GUILTY?

M Y MIND, IN DEPRESSION-ANXIETY mode, gravitates to guilt. Past wrongs I've done loom large in my life. Even good sermons sound like, "You ought to have been or done better; you should be or do better; shame on you."

I'm not talking about real guilt for which there is a solution. It's essential to face the sin which the Holy Spirit points out. We can repent of sin and confess it to God. Then we can look to 1 John 1:9—"If we confess our sins, he is faithful and just and will forgive us our sins and purify us from all unrighteousness." God keeps His promises, so that takes care of the actual guilt.

False guilt wallows in regrets and manufactures "should do's" or "ought to be's." My mind gets busy with these thoughts, and my spiritual vision gets blurred. Then, I don't see the accurate and current sins I need to confess and repent of. And that kind of thinking gets my focus off Jesus and onto me. Then, I start expecting myself to do what only He can do. So—more burden, more depression, more anxiety.

But there is hope at the end of this valley. And, much as I feared there wouldn't be, there was an end. When one is down in the valley, though, a prayer from Psalm 86 ministers to the soul:

O loving Lord, You abound in love. You are forgiving and good. Hear me, Lord. Listen as I cry for mercy. I call to You in trouble because You answer me. There is no one like You among the gods. You are the only one who can do the great things You do. You alone are God! I will praise You with everything I am! I will glorify You forever. Amen. (Psalm 86:5–8, 12 my paraphrase).

Next Step: Do you have trouble with guilt when your heart is anxious? Write down one thing you feel guilty about and surrender it to the Lord.

Prayer: O Lord, who abounds in love, thank You for forgiving my sin and leading me out of false guilt. Amen.

7

HEALING CAN BEGIN

A JOURNAL ENTRY IN the valley:

Dear Lord, I wish others would deal with these fearful thoughts for me, but I guess they can't. Please forgive me for seeking other people instead of looking to You. Only You can help (Psalm 62:5–6). I am Your child (1 John 3:1). You have chosen me for Your own (Colossians 3:12). I will praise and love You with all my heart.

The feelings of panic aren't so bad this morning, but fear and shame tumble in. I slept an extra hour today. I felt afraid to face the day. I'm worried I won't finish everything I need to do, and I would feel awful about that.

In our times, many Christians face persecution, loss of loved ones, lack of necessities, etc., and here I am—afraid to do household chores, write some checks, and make phone calls because I might not get it all done. "Shame on me," I think.

When I consider Scriptures like Hebrews 12:2 ("Keeping our eyes on Jesus") and Colossians 3:1–2 ("Seek what is above where Christ is.... Set your mind on things above"), all I can think about is that I haven't been doing that, so shame on me again.

Jesus, what are You saying to me when I get into these disturbed thinking patterns?

Maybe You are saying, "Don't be ashamed. Just repent and turn back to Me. Trust in Me. Let your body and mind rest so healing can begin."

I've come a long way since I wrote these things, and God does help me learn to rest so I can begin to heal. "Return to your rest, my soul, for the Lord has been good to you" (Psalm 116:7).

Next Step: Consider your thinking patterns. Write down the ones that keep you agitated and unable to rest. Consider how you could redirect your thinking.

Prayer: *Oh Lord, You have indeed been good to me. I come to You again for hope and rescue! You alone are my rock and stronghold. All praise belongs to You. Amen.*

8

YOU CAN CHOOSE

"**Y**OU'RE PUTTING YOUR FEELINGS above God," my friend said.

"Well, I don't want to do that. How can I put God at the top?"

"You trust what God says instead of what your feelings tell you. Your feelings lie to you. They say you're in danger, but you aren't. They say God isn't caring for you, but He is."

"You mean I can just choose?" I asked.

"Of course you can. You've been doing it all your life. For example, you chose to believe that the Bible is the Word of God, so you trust what it says."

The conversation ended, and I pondered, "Can I just decide to listen to God rather than what my body and mind tell me?" Yes. I can continue to believe the lies my feelings tell me and remain a victim. Or I can believe what God says (the truth) and progress toward recovery. God says He's caring for me and that I'm not in danger.

"I love the Lord, for he heard my voice; he heard my cry for mercy. ... The Lord is gracious and righteous; our God is full of compassion. ... Return to your rest, my soul ..." (Psalm 116:1, 5, 7).

I will believe in God's love. Then, my soul can rest because I remember God's goodness and presence as I trust His love. I choose to believe what He says instead of listening to the lying anxiety feelings. In Romans 15:13, Paul blesses his readers by asking the "God of hope" to fill them with joy and peace as they believe. Then, the power of the Holy Spirit will cause them to overflow with hope.

Next Step: What feelings or fears do you have that seem more accurate than the truth you know? Write them down. Then, talk about them to a Christian counselor or trusted friend who will help you distinguish truth from lies.

Prayer: Loving Father, thank You for this friend who reminded me that I could choose to believe and trust You even when the lies bombard my brain.

9

PRAYERS IN THE VALLEY

IN MY JOURNEY THROUGH the Valley of Anxiety, I struggled through sleepless nights and shaky days, and regrets often surfaced. One day, I wrote this prayer:

Dear Lord, You are God, the only God. You are the One who has ultimate control. I want to fit into Your plans, for they are good. You have always been faithful to me. Please forgive me for the times I've turned away and looked longingly at what I thought might have been or what used to be. Too often, I've run after what looked good from a human perspective instead of trusting Your goodness. Please forgive and cleanse as You have promised (1 John 1:9).

Holy God, I remember that You created us in Christ Jesus to do good works, which You prepared for us to do (Ephesians 2:10). And I feel so ashamed of the many times I've missed opportunities to do those good things. Lord God, please work in me to want to and then act according to Your purpose (Philippians 2:13). Then I can take advantage of the opportunities that You give me today instead of missing them and tomorrow wallowing in regret. Amen.

We can leave our regrets behind and trust God to work in us today to want and act according to His purpose.

In his song, "I Did It My Way," Frank Sinatra sang that his regrets were few and not worth mentioning. I find that odd because my regrets multiply when I've "done it my way" instead of God's. What about you?

Next Step: Write down a few regrets that have troubled you. What can you tell yourself so that you can leave these behind?

Prayer: God, my Savior, may I watch to take advantage of the opportunities You give me daily. Amen.

10

LEARNING IN THE STRUGGLE

WHEN MY ANXIETY SYMPTOMS intensified, I reached out for help. Through a series of misunderstandings, I spent a night in a "suicide watch" unit, even though suicide has never been an issue with me.

But while I was there, I met a young mother who had tried to take her own life. I talked with her but couldn't think of what to say. Her voice sounded flat, and I saw hopelessness in her eyes. I wished I knew how to help her. Later, I included her in my prayers. "Father, I wish she could grasp how much You love her and how precious she is to You. If she could understand how faithful and mighty You are and how You are for her and not against her, maybe she could find hope for living. Please help her."

When I went through my storm of anxiety, my troubled mind latched onto doubts and let the truth slip out of my hands. I wrote verses in my journal like these: "For we know how dearly God loves us because he has given us the Holy Spirit to fill our hearts with His love" (Romans 5:5 NLT), and "This I know: God is on my side!" (Psalm 56:9 NLT). Still, I felt unable to trust and believe the truth.

Doubt pointed at me and whined, "These things are true for others, but maybe not for me. I don't have as much faith as other people. I might not love

God enough, or perhaps I'm not good enough. There could be conditions on these promises that I'm not meeting."

Understanding that I could learn to think differently helped me. After the medicine started to calm the symptoms, I began to turn my gaze away from me and more to God. I realized that He is fantastic enough to make up for whatever I lack. He calls me to believe, trust, and rest in Him.

Next Step: Try this experiment: Write down Psalm 56:9 (above) or another encouraging verse. Read it aloud. Remind yourself of its truth. Do this often for the next three weeks, rejecting any contradictory thoughts. This exercise will increase your hope.

Prayer: *Dear Father, please help me remember that You love me and are for me. Amen.*

11

TOO LATE?

T WISTED THOUGHTS AND FEARS aggravated my anxiety in the journey toward wholeness. I suspected that I hadn't lived the life God gave me very well. I'd been tangled in self-focus and tripped up by mixed motives and other things displeasing to the Lord. I feared that now it was too late, and I was too old for God to use me.

I argued with anxiety. "Moses was eighty years old when he started leading the people of Israel. Surely one is never too old or too young to serve Jesus." But neither my trembling body with its sweaty palms nor my panicky mind seemed to be listening to my logic.

I asked God what to say to these thoughts and fears. He revealed that they were lies. God's promises in His Word contradict these mental messages.

Psalm 92:14 says that the righteous will stay "fresh and green" and "will still bear fruit in old age." And I am one of the righteous in Christ (2 Corinthians 5:21).

And Jesus says in John 15:16, "I chose you and appointed you so that you might go and bear fruit—fruit that will last."

Finally, Hebrews 4:7 reminds me, "*Today*, if you hear his voice, do not harden your hearts" (emphasis mine).

It's not too late! It's still today. Let's not let our hearts get hard. Let's choose to listen to God and believe and obey Him today.

Next Step: I felt like I had failed at life. Do you ever feel that way? Write down a couple of Bible verses, such as Lamentations 3:23 (God's compassions are new every morning), that will encourage you in those times.

Prayer: Thank You, Jesus, for appointing me to go and bear lasting fruit. Thank you that it's not too late for me to fit into Your plans, and You've given me today to serve You. Amen.

12

A Stepping Stone Out of the Valley

O UR HEAVENLY FATHER SENT help. He gave me "stepping stones" amid the muck of physical symptoms, doubts, and fears in Anxiety Valley. These Scripture verses, songs, and other help didn't make me feel less anxious for long, but they helped me overcome the painful days of struggle.

Music, including hymns I've loved for years, soothed my soul. I can sing many of them by heart, but I have a few hymnals at home from which I can sing. One favorite reminds me that I can find rest as I draw near God, "Near to the Heart of God":

Verse 1

"There is a place of quiet rest near to the heart of God.

A place where sin cannot molest, near to the heart of God."

Refrain

"O Jesus blest Redeemer, sent from the heart of God,

Hold us who wait before Thee near to the heart of God."[1]

---

1. *By Cleland B. McAfee; Public Domain*

During the summer of 1988, when the panic increased daily, I enjoyed singing along with audio tapes by Betty Jean Robinson. As I sang, the panic subsided, and I could return to normal activities.

Technology has moved far beyond the days of audio tapes since then. In my recent bout with panic, I listened to my favorite country gospel songs in my notebook computer with calming results.

Next Step: Write down a song or two that comes to mind that quiets your anxious heart. As you continue your journey, notice that God often provides songs that speak especially to you. Write those down as well. Then, when you can, create a playlist of those songs to help you when needed, or you can use it to encourage someone else. Appendix 2 lists songs that ministered to me.

Prayer: *Thank You, Lord, for Your gifts of music and song. Amen.*

13

SURE FOOTING

G OD OFFERED SPOTS OF sure footing as I hiked through my valley of anxiety. Here are a few:

My enemies say, "There is no help for her in God." If there is no help in You, then there is no hope. Only You can help. But indeed, there is hope and help in You, Lord. You are almighty, and Your Word is accurate. Your Word says You love me and will help me (Psalm 3:2–5).

I feel powerless, but I'm not. God has given me a spirit of power, love, and a sound mind (2 Timothy 1:7). If I walk by the Spirit, I can gain victory.

I am in the hands of the Lord God Almighty, Maker of heaven and earth. Nothing can pry me loose from His hands (John 10:28–29). My failures, sins, and poor choices cannot loosen God's grip on me. When fears or insecurity block my view of God, He is still here (Psalm 139:7–10).

I need to believe what God says rather than what fears, doubts, and feelings say. My anxiety feelings are lying to me. They don't change the truth of God's Word. The fears and doubts are lies. The "what-ifs" are lies. I will stand on the truth.

This was my prayer: Lord, Your delayed answer is better than the quick-fix answer I want now. Your ways are always better than ours, so help me to trust

You and Your love and mercy and to wait for the best answer. Please help me believe You are holding me up even though it doesn't feel like You are.

Next Step: Write down two spots of sure footing you have found to help you through your valleys. Share them with someone who might receive hope from your discoveries.

Prayer: Thank You for these thoughts and Scriptures that help me steady my shaky steps, merciful Father and God of all comfort (2 Corinthians 1:3).

14

HOPE IN GOD

A S MY JOURNEY CONTINUED, I journaled about my feelings. In mid-January, I wrote:

The hours and days pass moment by moment, and I feel faithless and fearful. I need sleep! I got very little last night. Lord, You are the One who sustains my body. You know what I need, and You determine how soon the meds will take effect. You are the One who gives sleep.

I seek You. I need You, Lord! You alone can help me. I don't feel faithful or trusting, but You alone are Lord, and I want to believe and trust You. Please heal my body and mind. Amen.

Journaling my prayers helped me sort through my thoughts and feelings.

When a godly friend prayed for me, I thought that would fix everything. I was disappointed that I still woke up every couple of hours at night and first thing in the morning in a panic. I also feared that I would disappoint her—as though I were responsible for producing the answer to her prayer.

Maybe I'm trusting in my ability to believe in God instead of trusting in God Himself. Father, I don't know how to change. Please help me focus on You and trust You. Amen.

The medicine finally started helping me sleep so I didn't wake up in panic mode each morning. It also enabled more reasonable ways of thinking. And God helped me change my thoughts to healthier patterns (Romans 12:2).

I encourage anyone still thrashing through the forest of anxiety or depression symptoms to keep hoping for God's help. He will lead you out of your distress at just the right time because His faithful love endures forever (1 Chronicles 16:34).

"Why, my soul, are you downcast? Why so disturbed within me? Put your hope in God, for I will yet praise him, my Savior and my God" (Psalm 42:5).

Next Step: Quiet yourself. Write about what you're thinking and feeling. Tell these things to God and wait for Him to speak to you. Write down any thoughts or Scriptures He brings to your mind.

Prayer: I praise You, God, my Savior, for You are good, and Your faithful love endures forever.

15

IN HIS HANDS

*J*ESUS, YOU KNOW ME, *and You walk and talk with me—in reality, not just imagination. You are indeed here. I want to trust in You. Please help me believe and trust You more. You gave me a good night's sleep last night to answer my prayer. Thank You. I want to be always grateful for all your good gifts.*

In anxious times, doubts attack. For example, this thought comes: "What if I'm just pretending that Jesus is right here with me, and He's not?" That's when I need to believe what God has said instead of what I'm feeling or thinking. Jesus says in Matthew 28:20, "And surely I am with you always, to the very end of the age."

Also, I feared that God expected me to do everything "right," and I wouldn't know what right was or how to do it. A song I heard helped me with this one. It reminded me that God is the One who saves me. I can cry out to Him. Paul says the same thing in Ephesians 2:8–9: "For it is by grace you have been saved, through faith—and this not from yourselves, it is the gift of God—not by works so that no one can boast."

To that, I respond, "Oh. Right. I'm not in charge. I don't have to be in control."

I remembered a hymn from my youth called "Higher Ground." * The second verse reads, "My heart has no desire to stay where doubts arise and fears dismay; though some may dwell where these abound, my prayer, my aim, is higher ground."[1] As I headed out of this valley, I asked to find the higher ground of peace.

Next Step: Find and write down a Bible verse, song, or inspirational writing that will comfort you when "doubts arise, and fears dismay."

Lord God Almighty, Maker of heaven and earth, it comforts me to remember that I'm in Your hands. Nothing can pry me loose. Not even my failures and poor choices can loosen Your grip on me. When doubt, fear, or self-focus blocks my view of You, You are still here. You don't quit loving me. You never give up on me.

Prayer: *Thank You, Lord, for Your everlasting, unbreakable love, which holds me up and gives me hope. Amen.*

---

1. *Text: Johnson Oatman, Jr.; Public Domain*

16

MAKING PROGRESS

A JOURNAL ENTRY FROM Anxiety Valley:

Another difficult night last night. Lord, You are my God. The truth is that You are here, that You love me, that I am Your child, and that You hear and answer my prayers.

But today, I'm having trouble believing the truth. The fear and the lies shout, and I don't feel Your presence. I struggle to hear Your voice. I want, yes—need—to know You and walk in a real relationship with You. Could I please have a sense of Your presence today? Would you show me how to enter Your secret place and hide under the shadow of Your wings (Psalm 91:1, 4)?

I wonder why I had so much trouble trusting the truth. Was it because my brain chemicals needed adjustment? Or maybe it was because I wanted to feel like those things were true. When I started telling myself that I could choose to believe the truth no matter what stuff seemed like or what my natural feelings were, I made progress.

The truth I needed to believe then and still need to trust is what I wrote in that journal entry—that God is here, that He loves me, that I am His child, and that He hears and answers my prayers.

As Moses told the people, "I call heaven and earth as witnesses against you today that I have set before you life and death, blessing and cursing. Therefore, choose life, so that you and your descendants may live" (Deuteronomy 30:19 BSB). To choose to believe the truth—that's life. To choose to accept the lies and how I feel—that's death. Jesus makes it possible for us to choose truth and life.

Next Step: Write down three truths that will encourage you as you begin to believe them.

Prayer: *Jesus, You said that You are the Truth and that the Holy Spirit leads us into all truth. I choose to believe You and what You say. Amen.*

17

A New Day

God has given me a new day, another chance to "follow the Holy Spirit in every part of my life" (Galatians 5:25 NLT), and I'm thankful. In the dark days of depression and panic, I didn't welcome the days as opportunities. Instead, I struggled through them, wishing I could feel better and fearing I never would. But finally, I did feel better. So, I can offer you hope that you will feel better too.

I continue to need medicine, but I do well if I take it. The "down" time was miserable, and I don't recommend such experiences to anyone. But looking back, I can see how God used it to boost my soul. It triggered a change in my thinking patterns to apply God's Word to my mind and my life more than I had in the past. My faith in Jesus has grown, and I walk with Him more closely than ever.

And now I can encourage those who still go through extra tough times with anxiety or depression with these thoughts: "Yes, you will get better. Maybe God is preparing a fresh start for you. Or He could be preparing you for something new. Whatever He's doing, I can assure you that God is working. We can trust Him."

Next Step: Write down some things you can thank God for about what you've gained through this journey through the valley.

Prayer: Thank You, Father, for today, another day to walk with Jesus and live for Him. Amen.

18

DANGER! COMPARISON QUICKSAND!

A MONG THE NOTES I made when I went through Anxiety Valley, I found these prayers:

In my distress, I cry out to You, Lord (Psalm 18:6). My thoughts and feelings say that my interaction with You is inferior to what others experience. I feel sure it must be my fault that I'm not connecting well with You, but I don't know how to do or be different. These thoughts grip me, and I struggle to break loose. The panic continues.

I see the source of some of my panic this morning—I compare myself to others and think of myself as "less than" and "failure."

Lord Jesus, please help me get my eyes on You, the Author and Finisher of my faith (Hebrews 12:2). Father, You have begun a good work in me and will continue until the day of Christ Jesus (Philippians 1:6). Please calm my anxious thoughts. Please help me anchor my mind in You (Isaiah 26:3).

Lord, I had thought that if I practiced certain devotional habits like reading my Bible more or praying more (or practicing them better), my spiritual life would look more like that of Christians I admire. But You are God, and You want a real relationship with me, not some imitation I try to conjure up by copying other saints.

From my current viewpoint on the other side of the valley, I can see that I had fallen into "comparison quicksand." I can also see that God threw out a plank to me in two of the Scriptures noted in my prayers: Hebrews 12:2 (BSB) ("Let us fix our eyes on Jesus, the author and perfecter of our faith.") and Isaiah 26:3 (NKJV) ("You will keep him in perfect peace, whose mind is stayed on You, because he trusts in You.")

Now, when I'm in a similar bog, I can grab that plank by getting my eyes off myself or other people and onto Jesus, and He can pull me out. This is easier said than done, but it is worth the work. Otherwise, I would continue to sink into the comparison quagmire.

Next Step: When are you tempted to compare yourself to others? Write down and memorize one of the verses above or a different verse that helps you. Use it to escape the quicksand next time you start to fall.

Prayer: *Thank You, God, for Your patience with this stubborn piece of clay!*

19

FREE FROM THE PIT

"THE ENEMY PURSUES ME, he crushes me to the ground; he makes me dwell in darkness like those long dead" (Psalm 143:3). Sometimes, the enemy pulls me into his pit of anger, resentment, criticism, and self-pity. These lead to and feed the depression I'm prone to.

Romans 12:2 tells me to change the way I think from my old way or the world's way to God's kingdom way. God will help and give me the grace to turn away from the enemy's thinking.

Then, I can work at putting Psalm 143:5–6 into practice. It says, "I remember the days of long ago; I meditate on all your works and consider what your hands have done. I spread out my hands to you; I thirst for you like a parched land."

I'll remember the "days of old—and how God has always been with me and had His hand on me no matter what. When we go through difficult moments, the Word tells us to remember what God has done for us. That gives us the courage to face today's difficulties. I'll meditate on what God has done and the wonders of creation.

I can choose to think about excellent and praiseworthy things, like God's goodness to each one of us, His love for every individual, and our right standing with Him, which He purchased with the blood of His own Son. Then, I'll seek to draw nearer to Him so He can satisfy my thirsty soul with His presence.

"For he satisfies the thirsty and fills the hungry with good things" (Psalm 107:9).

Next Step: If the weather permits, take a walk outside. Thank God for the air you breathe and for natural things you can see, such as grass, trees, sun, and clouds. If you can't go outside, think about the beautiful bodies God has given us and the intelligence and creativity He has given humanity. Then, take a few moments to write a prayer of thanksgiving to God for these things in your journal.

Prayer: *Faithful and creative Father, I praise You for Your greatness and thank You for Your love. Amen.*

20

I Believe—Help My Unbelief

W HILE I WAS STILL journeying through Anxiety/Depression Valley, I
wrote in my journal:

Lord, You told the Israelites that You would help them, strengthen them, and
hold them up with Your victorious right hand (Isaiah 41:10). Does that promise
apply to me also? All Your promises are "yes and amen" in Jesus (2 Corinthians
1:20), and I am in Jesus.

Thank You, Father, for helping me fight the fear and doubt. You are helping
me believe You and not feelings. I wonder if I believe You are helping or hoping
You will. Whichever it is, I want to believe and trust You anyway. You are
strengthening me. Please help me believe.

When my mind gets well, will it be easier to believe You? I hope I will *feel* like
my belief is genuine and not just something I'm pretending to myself.

In Mark 9:17–26, we read the account of a father who brought his son to
Jesus for healing. He pleaded with Jesus, "...But if you can do anything, take
pity on us and help us."

Jesus replied, "If you can? Everything is possible for him who believes."

Then the father exclaimed, "I do believe; help me overcome my unbelief!"

That was my request: "I do believe, Jesus. Help me believe more!"

Now that I'm on the other side of that valley, I know the answer to my question—YES. Believing and trusting God with a stable, healthy mind requires less effort. So, I offer you hope. When you travel beyond this troubled time, and you will go beyond it, your healthy mind will again grasp the truth.

Next Step: In what area do you need help believing? Write it down, and ask Jesus to help you today.

Prayer: *Thank You, Jesus, for healing my mind, body, and emotions. Thank You also for providing the daily capsule to keep my mind stable. Amen.*

21

NEEDING PEACE

"I FEEL SO STRESSED out!" My friend sobbed. "Pain and troubles tangle together, and I don't know which way to turn."

I understood. Her words reminded me of a difficult day when I felt the same way.

You've undoubtedly heard about how to eat an elephant—one bite at a time. It reminds us that we can do things better by attempting small tasks and eventually reaching the desired end.

But that day, I felt like the elephant had sat down on me, and its weight kept me immobilized.

Emotionally and spiritually overwhelmed, I couldn't think straight and misunderstood situations and people. The problems piled up before I could sort out my thoughts and feelings.

Nevertheless, I needed to deal with one thing at a time, trusting God to lead me through the tangled mess. I asked for prayer to regain my composure. Then I looked at one difficulty—my anger at a couple of people I felt had mistreated me.

I can't change what other people do, but I can choose how I process the emotional pain caused by others. I can remain angry and become bitter and depressed. That stirs up the flight or fight hormones, resulting in stress to both body and mind. Or, instead, I can seek God's help so I can forgive from my heart and find peace amid my pain.

Next Step: Write down some things you can do when life slams you from several directions at once.

Prayer: Lord Jesus, when my mind feels all tangled up, please lead me beside quiet waters (Psalm 23:2) where we can sort things out. Amen.

22

PAIN TO PEARLS

FROM NOVEMBER 2016 THROUGH March 2017, I journeyed through a dark valley of anxiety and depression. God showed Himself faithful throughout that "low road." Here's one insight I gained from the valley:

Pearls develop in an oyster or mussel as a substance called nacre coats an irritant in layers. A grain of sand or shell can act as a pearl starter. As I receive God's grace in life's troubles, it becomes like the nacre to coat the sorrow and hurt, one layer at a time, creating pearls.

Making pains into life pearls takes both Jesus and me. Jesus's part is to lead, guide, and give grace (wisdom and power) for dealing with life His way. My part is to follow Him step by step, day by day, living for Him and not myself.

I could return to my old ways—running from difficulties, wallowing in self-pity, or blaming others. Those and similar actions lead to more trouble, not pearl creation. Or I can humble myself and pray, believing God will hear and help. He will give me more and more grace (James 4:6).

One reason for rejoicing when I encounter various trials (James 1:2) is that those troubles may be pearl "seeds." The patience they work in me may be the first layer of "nacre" (grace). The very problem I'm facing may be the irritant that begins a beautiful and valuable pearl.

Next Step: Write down how you typically respond to difficulties. Does your reaction lead to more hope or more discouragement? If discouragement, what is one small step you can take today to change your response to trouble?

Prayer: Gracious Father, as I humbly pray to You, I believe You hear me and give me the grace I need. Please help me to be patient in trouble. Amen.

23

THINKING ABOUT THOUGHTS

HOW OFTEN MY THOUGHTS flit from here to there and all around during the day! I find myself going over conversations or actions, thinking about what I should or shouldn't have said or done. Maybe I think of what I should do "next time." Or I might plan what I'll do if such and such happens or if so and so does this or that.

But I have hope. Since I'm in Christ, old things have died, and new things have come (2 Corinthians 5:17). I have received the Holy Spirit, who gives me the power to get rid of the old me and put on the new self in Christ.

When I catch myself thinking the old way, I can tell myself to reject negative focus and pay attention to the task at hand. Or if the job doesn't take much thought (like combing my hair or vacuuming), I can meditate on a Bible verse I've been trying to memorize. After all, God's people are blessed when we meditate on Scripture (Psalm 1:2). Perhaps I could think about heaven, all Jesus has done for us, or God's love and grace.

Then, as I focus on the good things and let go of the scattered thoughts, I find myself relaxing and receiving peace in my soul.

Next Step: Think about your thoughts. Write a note on the journal page about uplifting thoughts you can choose instead of the old thoughts that drag you down.

Prayer: Holy Spirit, please help me keep my mind set on heavenly things instead of earthly things, as Colossians 3:2 directs. Then, I can live in Your peace. Amen.

24

THOUGHT REPLACEMENT THERAPY

J ESUS TOLD US TO bring every thought captive to obey Jesus Christ
(2 Corinthians 10:5). But how can I do that? My thinking patterns
have become knotted and twisted around experiences, people, and natural
tendencies.

I can drag the whole bundle to Jesus. He shows me loose ends protruding
from the tangles when I do that.

Then the Holy Spirit and I pull one free from the bunch, straighten it out,
and make it obey Christ. For example, I don't need to hold onto a bad attitude
about some disappointed expectation. When I start to stew, I can say to myself,
"No. That's the old way. I'm new in Christ (2 Corinthians 5:17). I'll let go of
the disappointment and rejoice in Him." And the next time I think about what
happened or didn't happen, I'll stop and remind myself that I'm rejoicing in the
Lord (Philippians 4:4).

When that thought thread is brought into submission, we can start pulling
on another one. We can begin untangling thoughts of blame and self-pity using
tools of humility and gratitude. In humility, I let go of blame and say, "Your will,
not mine, Lord." With a grateful heart, I turn my eyes away from myself and see
God's abundance of mercy and grace.

Next Step: Ask the Holy Spirit to show you one tangled thought pattern that He could help you untangle today. Write it down and watch for opportunities for Him to help you with it.

Prayer: Father, thank You for helping me learn more of Your Holy Spirit's work on my thought patterns.

25

VALUE IN THE VALLEY

C AN ANY GOOD COME from overwhelming panic feelings? Yes, but you couldn't have convinced me of that when I struggled with them daily for a few months. One day, I wrote in my journal:

"In your unfailing love, silence my enemies; destroy all my foes, for I am your servant" (Psalm 143:12).

Lord, I wake up each night in panic after sleeping only two hours. And when I get back to sleep, I wake up again in about two hours. Then, I wake up each morning in panic. I try to hold onto Your unfailing love and faithfulness, but the fears overwhelm me. Please help me!

Then, three hours later, I wrote:

The anxiety continues to overwhelm me. I remember some lines from a modern Christian song about not giving up. The singer reminds us to give our cares to God (1 Peter 5:7).

"So how do I give this to You, Lord?"

I'm unsure I received an answer, but I raised my hands and said, *"I give this anxiety to You." I still feel anxious. But maybe my feelings are lying to me again."*

Today, on my journey, I can see that God worked in my heart in that time of misery. He prepared the soil. He planted seedlings, such as greater humility and deeper trust in Him. Since those months of difficulty, I have seen God's seedlings grow. Patience flowers bloom. Fruits of joy develop.

I encourage you also, as a fellow follower of Jesus, that you can know God is working. He will bring you through this wilderness, even as He has brought many others through their rough seasons.

Next Step: Write a prayer to God expressing your anxieties and cares. Ask Him to help you let them go.

Prayer: *Thank You, God, for always working in ways I can't see. Amen.*

26

STILL LEARNING

D AY BY DAY, I'M still learning on this journey toward wholeness. I struggle with lessons in many areas, including corralling wild thoughts. Thankfully, God keeps working with me.

The "wild thoughts" don't cause as big a problem now as they used to generate. Back then, one thought triggered others, which went in a dozen different directions—all scary or sad.

I remember a phrase from 2 Corinthians 10:5 (NASB), "taking every thought captive to the obedience of Christ." The New Living Translation puts the expression into these words: "We capture their rebellious thoughts and teach them to obey Christ." I couldn't seem to capture my rebellious, tangled thinking. But I'm learning.

Cultivating thankfulness in my heart points my thoughts in the right direction. Medicine helps. Focusing on verses or passages of the Bible helps. Also, putting the ideas on paper aids in sorting them out and roping them in.

And just speaking the thought or thoughts out loud and praying. *Jesus, I'm bringing this thought (these thoughts) captive to You. Please help me now to think about things that are true, honorable, right, pure, lovely, admirable, excellent, or praiseworthy" (Philippians 4:8).* This makes a difference sometimes too.

Next Step: Write about ways to focus, which you might use when your thoughts seem to jump onto a hamster wheel.

Prayer: God our Father, thank You for helping me continue to learn on my journey through this life. Thank You for continuing Your work in my heart without giving up. Amen.

27

GOD AS OUR REFUGE

AT ONE POINT DURING the years between two major depression episodes, my husband experienced a severe head injury, and we didn't know if he would live.

One thing that comforted me through that scary time was remembering that God made heaven and earth (Psalm 121:2) and that He would help us. (My husband completely recovered. Praise God!)

At times like that, meditating on God as my strength and refuge helped me find peace. He alone is God (Psalm 46:10). Nothing happens that's too difficult for Him to handle.

I wrote this prayer after the second depressive episode as I moved toward wholeness:

Lord Jesus, I want to hide myself in You as my Refuge. My attackers aren't usually physical. Instead, they frequently come as sneaky, ugly thoughts that drag me into fear and anger. Sometimes, they've lured me into going my way instead of trusting You. Your armor protects me in battle, but sometimes, I need to rest in the safety of Your shelter. I watch in hope for You, Lord. People fail, but You never do. I fail, but my life is hidden with Christ in You. You are my refuge and hiding place and shelter. I praise You, my Hope.

Next Step: What kind of trouble do you need God's help with today? Write a prayer asking Him for His help and thank Him because He hears you (Micah 7:7).

Prayer: *I wait for You, God my Savior. You hear and answer my prayers. I will keep my eyes on You. Amen.*

28

HOPE IN JESUS

"I TRY TO TAKE one day at a time, but lately several days have attacked me at once," the poster said. I laughed because sometimes it seems like life is like that. On those days, I can meditate on Psalm 146:5–6 (BSB):

"Blessed is he whose help is the God of Jacob, whose hope is in the Lord his God, the Maker of heaven and earth, the sea, and everything in them. He remains faithful forever."

When I get discouraged, I must tell myself, "Self, hope in the Lord our God who made heaven and earth. Let disappointment go and trust God to work all for my good and His glory. O my soul, don't look to others for hope or think that more possessions will fill this need. Let God satisfy you. Trust His wisdom, not your own. Remember, soul, that you find rest in God alone and that your victory comes from Him (Psalm 62:1). Hope and trust in Jesus the Messiah."

I could also think about Isaiah 40:31, which tells me that I renew my strength when I wait on the Lord. I needed power that August day years ago when I went to the hospital. I could barely put one foot in front of the other. Of course, meditating on Scripture wasn't enough back then, but as I progressed toward wholeness, the Scriptures offered needed assistance.

Next Step: Write down a sentence or two of self-talk based on Scripture to help you hope. Think about it and repeat it several times for the next few days.

Prayer: O Lord our God, You are always near us and hear and answer prayer. You love and care for each of us with love higher and broader than the heavens above and deeper than the ocean. I stand amazed by such love. May I remember Your love and presence when I begin to slip into hopelessness. Amen.

29

BEGINNING TO END

W HEN DID I BEGIN this journey toward peace? I thought it began in early November of 2016 when panic started interfering in everyday life, but I've been on the trip all my Christian life. Even my experiences in 1988 were part of the journey.

Likewise, I thought it ended by the first part of March of 2017 when the anxiety had subsided, and I felt good, but again, my walk toward wholeness won't end until my life on earth is complete and I see Jesus face to face.

John writes in his first letter, "Dear friends, now we are children of God, and what we will be has not yet been made known. But we know that when Christ appears, we shall be like him, for we shall see him as he is" (1 John 3:2).

Nevertheless, during those four months, I struggled with the brokenness of anxiety and depression in a way that made that part of the journey particularly noticeable. So, how can I encourage others who find themselves on the same road?

If you're a follower of Christ yet feel overwhelmed with anxiety or depression, rest assured that God is with you. I know it isn't easy. I was so wrapped up in fear that I had trouble believing God was with me.

Verbal reminders from friends and in sermons helped me. Many Scriptures tell us this truth, but I wavered in unbelief because I couldn't *feel* God's presence. I hope you'll do better at believing than I did, but even if you don't, He's still with you, loving and helping you through it all. And He will still be with you when you come out on the other side.

How do I know? First, because God has promised and is faithful (Hebrews 10:23). Second, because of what God did for me. How thankful I am for God's faithfulness and patience with me!

"God has said, 'Never will I leave you; never will I forsake you.' So we say with confidence, 'The Lord is my helper; I will not be afraid. What can mere mortals do to me?'" (Hebrews 13:5–6)

Next Step: If you are going through a valley of anxiety or depression, what has encouraged you to keep moving toward peace? Write some words of encouragement to your future self so they are available when discouragement tries to overwhelm you.

Prayer: Father, when I get discouraged, please help me trust that You are with me. Amen.

30

PROGRESS BEYOND THE VALLEY

WHEREVER WE ARE ON our journey, we can go forward. As we move ahead, we can look to God for the hope He offers as we travel through and beyond the valleys of anxiety and depression.

God offers hope, not easy or quick answers like I often want. I wanted a magic wand answer, but God led me instead through the struggles I've shared in this book. He knew that I needed to learn the lessons there. He also knew I needed to share them with you.

The medicine I still require reminds me that God has made us unique. Some can get well without medication. Others, like me, will probably always need it.

Each person differs in experience. Some suffer from anxiety and depression, others from one or the other, and others never have problems with either.

Experiences differ from time to time as well. The first bout I had with depression was characterized by constant crying and fear, along with physical symptoms. My most recent trouble involved more sleeplessness, trembling, and panic.

So, take courage, my friend. You will get well. You're not alone. Seek human help when you need it. And remember that God is with you and will never fail or forsake you.

Next Step: Evaluate where you are on your journey toward peace. Are you still struggling, or have you come to a calm spot? Ask God what your next step should be. Listen, and write down the thoughts He brings to your mind.

Prayer: *And now I pray for you, as Paul prayed for the Roman believers, "that God, the source of hope, will fill you completely with joy and peace because you trust in him. Then you will overflow with confident hope through the power of the Holy Spirit" (Romans 15:13 NLT).*

APPENDIX 1

SCRIPTURE REFERENCES

Devotion 1 – Hope Amid Anxiety

"My soul, wait only upon God and silently submit to Him; for my hope and expectation are from Him" (Psalm 62:5, AMPC).

Devotion 2 – A Ray of Hope

"Why, my soul, are you downcast? Why so disturbed within me? Put your hope in God, for I will yet praise him, my Savior and my God" (Psalm 42:11).

Devotion 3 – God Will Lift You Up

"Humble yourselves, therefore, under God's mighty hand, that he may lift you up in due time" (1 Peter 5:6).

Devotion 4 – A Journey Begins

"We wait in hope for the Lord; he is our help and our shield. In him our hearts rejoice, for we trust in his holy name. May your unfailing love be with us, Lord, even as we put our hope in you" (Psalm 33:20–22).

"But blessed is the man who trusts in the Lord, whose confidence is in him" (Jeremiah 17:7).

Devotion 5 – God Sends Comfort

"The Lord is good, a refuge in times of trouble. He cares for those who trust in Him" (Nahum 1:7).

"The Lord is gracious and righteous; our God is full of compassion. ... Return to your rest, my soul, for the Lord has been good to you" (Psalm 116:5, 7).

"But to all who believed him and accepted him, he gave the right to become children of God. They are reborn—not with a physical birth resulting from human passion or plan, but a birth that comes from God" (John 1:12–13 NLT)

"I give them eternal life, and they shall never perish; no one will snatch them out of my hand. My Father, who has given them to me, is greater than all; no one can snatch them out of my Father's hand" (John 10:28–29).

"God has said, 'Never will I leave you; never will I forsake you'" (Hebrews 13:5).

Devotion 6 – Guilty or Not Guilty?
"If we confess our sins, he is faithful and just and will forgive us our sins and purify us from all unrighteousness" (1 John 1:9).

Devotion 7 – Healing Can Begin
"Yes, my soul, find rest in God; my hope comes from him. Truly he is my rock and my salvation; he is my fortress, I will not be shaken" (Psalm 62:5–6).

"See what great love the Father has lavished on us, that we should be called children of God! And that is what we are! The reason the world does not know us is that it did not know him" (1 John 3:1).

"Therefore, as God's chosen people, holy and dearly loved, clothe yourselves with compassion, kindness, humility, gentleness and patience" (Colossians 3:12).

"Let us fix our eyes on Jesus, the author and perfecter of our faith, who for the joy set before him endured the cross, scorning its shame, and sat down at the right hand of the throne of God" (Hebrews 12:2 BSB).

"Since, then, you have been raised with Christ, set your hearts on things above, where Christ is seated at the right hand of God. Set your minds on things above, not on earthly things" (Colossians 3:1–2).

Devotion 8 – You Can Choose

"I love the Lord, for he heard my voice; he heard my cry for mercy. ... The Lord is gracious and righteous; our God is full of compassion. ... Return to your rest, my soul, for the Lord has been good to you." (Psalm 116:1, 5, 7).

"May the God of hope fill you with all joy and peace as you trust in him, so that you may overflow with hope by the power of the Holy Spirit" (Romans 15:13).

Devotion 9 – Prayers in the Valley

(1 John 1:9—See Devotion 6 above.)

"For we are God's handiwork, created in Christ Jesus to do good works, which God prepared in advance for us to do" (Ephesians 2:10).

"For it is God who works in you to will and to act in order to fulfill his good purpose" (Philippians 2:13).

Devotion 10 – Learning in the Struggle

"For we know how dearly God loves us, because He has given us the Holy Spirit to fill our hearts with His love" (Romans 5:5 NLT).

"This I know: God is on my side" (Psalm 56:9 NLT).

Devotion 11 – Too Late?

"They will still bear fruit in old age, they will stay fresh and green" (Psalm 92:14).

"God made him who had no sin to be sin for us, so that in him we might become the righteousness of God" (2 Corinthians 5:21).

"You did not choose me, but I chose you and appointed you to go and bear fruit—fruit that will last—and so that whatever you ask in my name the Father will give you" (John 15:16).

"God again set a certain day, calling it 'Today.' This he did when a long time later he spoke through David, as in the passage already quoted: 'Today, if you hear his voice, do not harden your hearts'" (Hebrews 4:7).

"Because of the Lord's great love we are not consumed, for his compassions never fail. They are new every morning; great is your faithfulness" (Lamentations 3:22–23).

Devotion 13 – Sure Footing

"Where can I go from your Spirit? Where can I flee from your presence? If I go up to the heavens, you are there; if I make my bed in the depths, you are there. If I rise on the wings of the dawn, if I settle on the far side of the sea, even there your hand will guide me, your right hand will hold me fast" (Psalm 139:7–10).

"Praise be to the God and Father of our Lord Jesus Christ, the Father of compassion and the God of all comfort" (2 Corinthians 1:3).

Devotion 14 – Hope in God

"Do not conform to the pattern of this world, but be transformed by the renewing of your mind. Then you will be able to test and approve what God's will is—his good, pleasing and perfect will" (Romans 12:2).

"Give thanks to the Lord, for he is good; his love endures forever" (1 Chronicles 16:34).

"Why, my soul, are you downcast? Why so disturbed within me? Put your hope in God, for I will praise him, my Savior and my God" (Psalm 42:5).

Devotion 15 – In His Hands
"And surely I am with you always, to the very end of the age" (Matthew 28:20).

"For it is by grace you have been saved, through faith—and this is not from yourselves, it is the gift of God—not by works, so that no one can boast" (Ephesians 2:8–9).

Devotion 16 – Making Progress
"He who dwells in the secret place of the Most High shall abide under the shadow of the Almighty. ... He shall cover you with His feathers, and under His wings you shall take refuge; His truth shall be your shield and buckler" (Psalm 91:1,4 NKJV).

"I call heaven and earth as witnesses against you today that I have set before you life and death, blessing and cursing. Therefore choose life, so that you and your descendants may live," (Deuteronomy 30:19 BSB).

Devotion 17 – A New Day
"Since we are living by the Spirit, let us follow the Spirit's leading in every part of our lives" (Galatians 5:25 NLT).

Devotion 18 – Danger! Comparison Quicksand!
"In my distress I called to the Lord; I cried to my God for help. From his temple he heard my voice; my cry came before him, into his ears" (Psalm 18:6).

"He who began a good work in you will carry it on to completion until the day of Christ Jesus" (Philippians 1:6).

"Let us fix our eyes on Jesus, the author and perfecter of our faith" (Hebrews 12:2 BSB).

"You will keep him in perfect peace, whose mind is stayed on You because he trusts in You" (Isaiah 26:3 NKJV).

Devotion 19 -Free from the Pit
"The enemy pursues me, he crushes me to the ground; he makes me dwell in darkness like those long dead" (Psalm 143:3).

"Do not conform to the pattern of this world, but be transformed by the renewing of your mind. Then you will be able to test and approve what God's will is—his good, pleasing and perfect will" (Romans 12:2).

"I remember the days of long ago; I meditate on all your works and consider what your hands have done. I spread out my hands to you; I thirst for you like a parched land" (Psalm 143:5–6).

"For he satisfies the thirsty and fills the hungry with good things" (Psalm 107:9).

Devotion 20 – I Believe—Help My Unbelief
"So do not fear, for I am with you; do not be dismayed, for I am your God. I will strengthen you and help you; I will uphold you with my righteous right hand" (Isaiah 41:10).

"For all the promises of God in Him are Yes, and in Him Amen, to the glory of God through us" (2 Corinthians 1:20 NKJV).

"Jesus asked the boy's father, 'How long has he been like this?' 'From childhood,' he answered. 'It has often thrown him into fire or water to kill him. But if you can do anything, take pity on us and help us.' 'If you can?' said Jesus. 'Everything is possible for one who believes.' Immediately the boy's father exclaimed, 'I do believe; help me overcome my unbelief!'" (Mark 9:21–24).

Devotion 21 – Needing Peace
"He makes me lie down in green pastures, he leads me beside quiet waters" (Psalm 23:2).

Devotion 22 – Pain to Pearls
"But he gives us more grace. That is why Scripture says: 'God opposes the proud but shows favor to the humble" (James 4:6).

"Consider it pure joy, my brothers and sisters, whenever you face trials of many kinds" (James 1:2).

Devotion 23 – Thinking about Thoughts
"Therefore, if anyone is in Christ, the new creation has come: The old has gone, the new is here!" (2 Corinthians 5:17).

"But his delight is in the law of the Lord, and on his law he meditates day and night" (Psalm 1:2).

"Set your minds on things above, not on earthly things" (Colossians 3:2).

Devotion 24 – Thought Replacement Therapy
"We demolish arguments and every pretension that sets itself up against the knowledge of God, and we take captive every thought to make it obedient to Christ" (2 Corinthians 10:5).

(2 Corinthians 5:17—See Devotion 23 above.)

"Rejoice in the Lord always. I will say it again: Rejoice!" (Philippians 4:4).

Devotion 25 – Value in the Valley

"In your unfailing love, silence my enemies; destroy all my foes, for I am your servant" (Psalm 143:12).

"Cast all your anxiety on him because he cares for you" (1 Peter 5:7).

Devotion 26 – Still Learning

"We destroy every proud obstacle that keeps people from knowing God. We capture their rebellious thoughts and teach them to obey Christ" (2 Corinthians 10:5 NLT).

"Finally, brothers and sisters, whatever is true, whatever is noble, whatever is right, whatever is pure, whatever is lovely, whatever is admirable—if anything is excellent or praiseworthy—think about such things" (Philippians 4:8).

Devotion 27 – God As Our Refuge

"My help comes from the Lord, the Maker of heaven and earth" (Psalm 121:2).

"Be still, and know that I am God; I will be exalted among the nations, I will be exalted in the earth" (Psalm 46:10).

"But as for me, I watch in hope for the Lord, I wait for God my Savior; my God will hear me" (Micah 7:7).

Devotion 28 – Hope in Jesus

"Blessed are those whose help is the God of Jacob, whose hope is in the Lord their God. He is the Maker of heaven and earth, the sea, and everything in them—he remains faithful forever" (Psalm 146:5–6).

"Truly my soul finds rest in God; my salvation comes from him" (Psalm 62:1).

"But those who hope in the Lord will renew their strength. They will soar on wings like eagles; they will run and not grow weary, they will walk and not be faint" (Isaiah 40:31).

Devotion 29 – Beginning to End

"Dear friends, now we are children of God, and what we will be has not yet been made known. But we know that when Christ appears, we shall be like him, for we shall see him as he is" (1 John 3:2).

"Let us hold unswervingly to the hope we profess, for he who promised is faithful" (Hebrews 10:23).

"Keep your lives free from the love of money and be content with what you have, because God has said, 'Never will I leave you; never will I forsake you.' So we say with confidence, 'The Lord is my helper; I will not be afraid. What can mere mortals do to me?" (Hebrews 13:5–6).

Devotion 30 – Progress Beyond the Valley

"I pray that God, the source of hope, will fill you completely with joy and peace because you trust in him. Then you will overflow with confident hope through the power of the Holy Spirit" (Romans 15:13 NLT).

APPENDIX 2

ENCOURAGING SONGS AND HYMNS

"Turn Your Eyes Upon Jesus" by Rosemary Siemens

"Why So Downcast O My Soul?" by Sonrise Church - Olympia WA

"Sweet Peace, the Gift of God's Love" by Lifebreakthrough CMA t.v

"Great Is Thy Faithfulness" by First Baptist Dallas

"How Firm a Foundation" by The Petersons

"Marvelous Grace" by SE Samonte

"Near to the Heart of God" by SE Samonte

"Ride Out Your Storm" by Betty Jean Robinson

"He Did for Me What I Could Not Do for Myself" by Carroll Robertson

"Higher Ground" by SE Samonte

"His Yoke is Easy" by Nehemiah Ryan

"Give Them All to Jesus" by Evie Tornquist

"God on the Mountain" by Betty Jean Robinson

"I Stand Amazed" by Rosemary Siemens

Some Final Thoughts

THE CONCEPTION OF THIS book followed our pastor's sermon about using the gifts God gave us for His glory. I felt God's nudge to do more with my writing than I had. I'd been writing my blog with one or two short monthly posts and felt pleased to do so.

Still, I wanted to obey God, so I took advantage of an advertisement about joining an online writing group. There, I made a few online friends who remain a blessing. However, I felt outclassed by the group leaders who had already published with traditional publishers. The large group seemed impersonal, and most members had more skill and knowledge than I.

So, I found a smaller, slower-paced online group and participated in some of their workshops. I met Andrea Lende at one of those workshops. She offered to help me create a book from my blog posts and gave me her phone number. I wrote the number in my notes and put it away for some possible future time.

Then, one day in my prayer time, I talked with God again about writing a book. I told Him it was too big a job, too complicated, and something professional writers did. How could an old, easily discouraged woman like me write a book?

Then God spoke to my heart. "I'm not asking you to write a book today; I'm just telling you to take the first step." In obedience to God, I called Andrea.

I took the second step by compiling excerpts from my blog about panic and depression. Step by step, I moved forward to write this book so you or someone with whom you share it can have the hope and help God gave me during my panic and depression episodes.

Your battle with depression, anxiety, or panic may seem like it won't end, but I believe it will. One step at a time, one day at a time, God will show you more about the beautiful life He has planned for you. You, too, will do the thing that you had no idea you could do.

ABOUT THE AUTHOR

God rescued and healed Tricia Opitz when she was trapped in debilitating anxiety and depression. She wrote this book to help others struggling with these mental and emotional disorders so that those with loved ones suffering from these disorders can glimpse their experiences.

Tricia writes short devotions for her blog on her website. She shares insights she discovered in Scripture to help others in their daily walk with Jesus. She chooses ten of these devotions every Christmas and creates a printed booklet to share with friends and family during the holiday season.

Besides writing, Tricia volunteers at a local food pantry/clothes closet. She's addicted to funny, clean jokes and has filled a tote box with ones she's collected over the years. Humor can be an excellent antidote to depression. Proverbs 17:22 reminds us that a cheerful heart helps like medicine.

Tricia, a retired school librarian, is a wife and mother of a daughter with a family. Her work as a librarian fostered her interest in reading and, eventually, writing. Tricia resides in a rural area of northeast Oklahoma.

You can contact Tricia on her website at www.triciajots4jesus.com

REVIEW ASK

If you enjoyed this book, please consider
reviewing it on Amazon so that more people
who need this message can easily find it!

Thank you for reading, and I hope
the words within these pages blessed you.

—Tricia Opitz

www.ingramcontent.com/pod-product-compliance
Lightning Source LLC
Chambersburg PA
CBHW071203120626
46546CB00006B/2399